A Visit to
GREECE

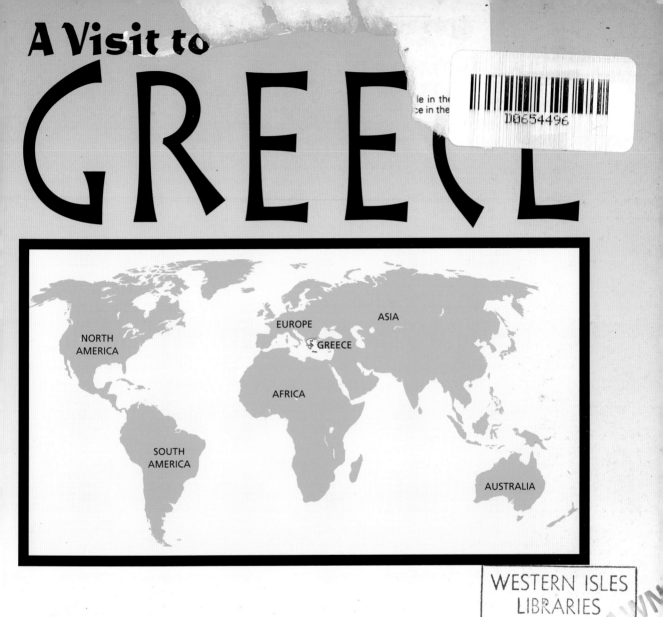

NORTH
AMERICA

EUROPE

ASIA

GREECE

AFRICA

SOUTH
AMERICA

AUSTRALIA

 eter & Connie Roop

Heinemann
LIBRARY

First published in Great Britain by Heinemann Library
Halley Court, Jordan Hill, Oxford OX2 8EJ
a division of Reed Educational and Professional Publishing Ltd.
Heinemann is a registered trademark of Reed Educational & Professional Publishing Limited.

OXFORD MELBOURNE AUCKLAND KUALA LUMPUR
SINGAPORE IBADAN NAIROBI KAMPALA JOHANNESBURG
GABORONE PORTSMOUTH NH CHICAGO

Designed by AMR
Illustrations by Art Construction
Printed in Hong Kong / China

02 01 00 99
10 9 8 7 6 5 4 3 2 1

ISBN 0 431 08323 1
This title is also available in a hardback library edition (ISBN 0 431 08314 2).

British Library Cataloguing in Publication Data

Roop, Peter
  A visit to Greece
  1. Greece – Social conditions – 1974 – – Juvenile literature
  2. Greece – Geography – Juvenile literature
  3. Greece – Social life and customs – 20th century – Juvenile literature
  I.Title II.Greece
  949.5·076

Acknowledgements
The Publishers would like to thank the following for permission to reproduce photographs:
J Allan Cash Ltd: pp6, 7, 8, 9, 10, 11, 18, 19, 21, 28; Hutchison Library: J Egan pp5, 16, R Giling
pp12, 23, 25, 29, S Molins p14, I Tree p13; Travel Ink: I Booth p17, N Bowen-Morris p26,
A Lewis p24; Trip: B North p15, H Rogers p20, V Sidoropolev p27, A Tovy p22

Cover photograph reproduced with permission of J Hartley, Panos Pictures

Any words appearing in bold, **like this**, are explained in the Glossary.

Contents

Greece

Key
- Land above 1000 m
- Land above 0 m/sea level
- ● Capital
- ● Important cities

Salonica

▲ Mt Olympus
2917 m

North

G R E E C E

Athens

MEDITERRANEAN SEA

Greece is the furthest south of all countries in **Europe**. Most of the **mainland** is surrounded by the Mediterranean Sea. It also has about 2000 islands of all sizes.

People live on only 160 of the islands.
The rest are too dry and rocky for people
to live on. Many people visit Greece for
its beautiful beaches.

Land

Mountains cover most of Greece.
The biggest ones lie in the middle of
Greece. There are a few small rivers,
but these dry up in the hot summer.

Most of the lower land is along the coasts. This is where many of the towns and cities are.

Landmarks

Mount Olympus is the highest mountain in Greece. Long ago, the Greeks believed that gods lived on the top of Mount Olympus.

Greece has many **ancient** buildings. The Parthenon is one of the most famous. It was built almost 2500 years ago as a **temple** for Athena, the goddess of Athens.

Homes

Athens and Salonica are the two biggest cities in Greece. One third of all Greeks live in or near Athens. Families live in small flats because the city is so crowded.

Most Greeks live in the country. Their homes usually have four or five rooms, flat roofs and white-washed walls. Some Greeks grow plants up the walls for the fruit and for decoration.

Food

The Greeks eat a lot of **seafood** from the Mediterranean Sea. Olive oil is used in much of the cooking. The main meat eaten is lamb.

Lunch is the main meal of the day, when all the family gets together. It is often followed by an afternoon nap away from the heat of the day.

Clothes

Most Greeks wear clothes like yours.
Some older Greeks wear black when
they go out. This is to show **respect** for
members of the family who have died.

The Greeks' **national** dress is a white shirt, red hat and white skirt. Men, women and children wear this for special celebrations and dances.

Work

Many Greeks are farmers. They grow wheat, tobacco, cotton, grapes and olives. They also keep sheep and goats for their milk which is made into yoghurt or cheese.

Many Greeks work in the **tourist** industry because there are so many visitors to their country. They work in hotels, restaurants, shops and transport.

Transport

People travel by **modern** and **old-fashioned** transport. In the country, many villages only have dirt tracks so donkeys are a good way of carrying heavy loads.

Greek shipping companies are famous around the world. Ships also ferry **tourists** between Greek islands or take them on cruises around the Mediterranean Sea.

Language

Most Greeks speak the Greek language.
Greek is the oldest language spoken in
Europe. Many Greeks also speak English.

Greek has its own alphabet of 24 letters. Many signs are written in both the Greek and **Roman** alphabets.

School

Greek children go to school from the age of 6 to 15. They learn maths, art, music, religion, history and physical education.

Greek is the main language taught in school. Many children learn English or French, too.

Free time

The Olympic Games were first held
in Greece, over 2000 years ago.
Today, almost all Greeks enjoy
football (soccer) and swimming.

The evening walk is a time for family and friends to chat. Adults also visit coffeehouses, called kafeneions, to play cards and meet their friends.

Celebrations

Easter is the most important festival. The Greeks celebrate many other **religious** festivals, too. Priests dress up in special robes and lead parades through the streets.

At some festivals, the Greeks dress up in **traditional** costumes and celebrate with dancing and singing.

The Arts

People have written and acted plays in Greece for over 2000 years. Today, both old and new plays are **performed** in the **ancient** theatres.

The bouzouki is a Greek string instrument.
Musicians play **traditional** songs on the
bouzouki which are happy and sad at the
same time.

Factfile

Name   The full name of Greece is the Hellenic Republic.

Capital   The **capital** city of Greece is Athens.

Languages   Most Greeks speak Greek and many can also speak a little English.

Population There are about $10\frac{1}{2}$ million people living in Greece.

Money   Instead of the dollar or pound, the Greeks have the drachma.

Religion   Most Greeks believe in Greek Orthodoxy which is part of the Christian church.

Products   Greece produces lots of olives and olive oil, cotton, grapes, tobacco, oil and some metals.

Words you can learn

enas (eh-nah)	one
dhio (theeoh)	two
tris (treace)	three
ya sis (yah-soos)	hello
andio (a-DEoh)	goodbye
efharisto (efkha-REE stoh)	thank you
parakalo (barata-LOH)	please
ne (neh)	yes
ohi (okhi)	no

Glossary

ancient	from a long time ago
capital	the city where the government is based
Europe	the collection of countries north of the Mediterranean Sea
mainland	a country's largest block of land
modern	new and up-to-date
national	shared by a nation or country
old-fashioned	from the past
performed	put on stage
religious	to do with people's beliefs
respect	to value someone or think highly of them
Roman	the type of letters which you read and write in English
seafood	fish and shellfish
temple	usually a very grand building used as a place of worship
tourist	a person who travels to other countries for holidays
traditional	the way something has been done or made for a long time

Index